Power Struggles

Successful Techniques for Educators

Discipline Associates
Rochester, New York
1997

About The Author

ALLEN N. MENDLER, Ph.D., is an educator, school psychologist and nationally known presenter on the topic of discipline and effective behavior management. Author of *What Do I Do When? How to Achieve Discipline with Dignity in the Classroom* and co-author of the ASCD yearbook, *Discipline with Dignity*, Dr. Mendler is in high demand as a national conference speaker and as a consultant to school systems throughout the United States and Canada. Publications include *Smiling at Yourself: Educating Young Children About Stress and Self-Esteem* and *Am I In Trouble?*

Library of Congress Catalog Card Number: 96-071316

ISBN: 0-9655115-2-9

*For the thousands of talented,
tireless educators
who make differences
in the lives of students every day
and receive too little
appreciation.
On behalf of hostile,
aggressive youngsters,
thank you for not giving up.*

Allen Mendler

TABLE OF CONTENTS

Introduction...1

On The Spot...3

A Three-Prong Approach.......................................4

Identifying The Problem.......................................6

What Does Work?..9

Prevention Strategies...11

Convey Warmth..11

Give Opportunities For Students To Be In Charge...........13

Be Respectful of Differences
In the Ways Students Learn..................................18

Intervention Strategies.......................................23

The Hostility Cycle...28

Substitute Less Powerful Words and Images................31

Activity For Reframing.......................................37

Learn and Use Defusing Strategies.........................38

Basic Defusing Skills...41

Specific Defusing Statements...............................47

Additional Steps That May Be Necessary 50

The Private Three-Step Technique...........................54

Dealing With the Rest of the Class.........................57

Power Struggle Scenarios....................................62

An Article: Classroom Counteraggression..................63

Bibliography...68

INTRODUCTION

Educators can no longer rely exclusively upon their stature and authority for effective discipline. A typical classroom includes students of considerable behavioral diversity with some having short fuses who anger easily, often without obvious provocation. They may say offensive things or act in hostile ways that trigger power struggles. Maintaining classroom focus on the achievement of educational goals is often dependent upon successfully managing disruptive moments. This practical handbook provides many specific strategies of prevention so that power struggles occur less often. It also includes easy-to-learn methods of effective intervention that work while preserving student and personal dignity. The strategies grow from the work of Curwin and Mendler's *Discipline With Dignity*. It is my hope that all educators find lots of helpful tips and advice throughout the book. Too much instructional time is currently lost because of minor disruptions that quickly escalate into class-room battles eroding relationships and respect.

As the emphasis of the book is on practical strategies that can be implemented at school, there is a relative absence of the guiding theoretical framework. Interested educators can refer to numerous prior publications listed in the bibliography for this information.

I'd like to thank my friend, colleague and frequent co-author, Rick Curwin, for his helpful suggestions in editing the manuscript.

ON THE SPOT

It is Phil's first day in Mr. Jones' special education resource class. This 15-year-old youth has recently left his residential treatment center where he spent a year in treatment due to a number of problems including active displays of hostility towards authority figures. On his first day, Phil arrives dressed completely in black, including black finger polish, make-up around his eyes and a bandanna. He is distantly quiet in class as Mr. Jones leads an academic discussion. Towards the very end of class, Mr. Jones says, "Phil, as a new student in our class, I am interested in your first impressions. Would you share any thoughts, ideas or impressions you have of the class?" Phil stares ahead and without changing expression, looks directly at Mr. Jones and says to him, "I think you like guys in tight pants." Some students become intensely quiet as they await Mr. Jones' response while others take on more of an "ooh- what are you going to do about it" posture. Jones takes a few deep breaths, scratches his head, looks directly at Phil and says, "Phil, I have been trying hard to get other students in this class to speak their minds. Here you are, a brand new student in this class, and on your very first day you showed us how. Now in all honesty, I'm not real thrilled about what you said, but I do appreciate your willingness to speak your mind." An hour later, without any prompting, Phil apologizes.

Although not all challenging moments end as successfully as this one, there are many things that educators can learn to say and do to defuse a power struggle as effectively as Mr. Jones. This book offers lots of specific ways of doing that.

A THREE-PRONG APPROACH

It is estimated that 70 to 80 percent of challenging student behavior in school is primarily attributable to outside factors such as dysfunctional families, violence in our culture, the effects of drugs and alcohol, and fragmented communities. Columnist Lorraine O'Connell reflects the sentiments of many when she writes:

"Personally, I'd like to see parents of wayward kids compelled to sport bumper stickers acknowledging parental incompetence:

I'm the spineless parent of kids who do whatever they want.

I'm the ineffectual parent of a convicted teenage felon.

I'm the ashamed parent of a pregnant

junior high student.

I'm the permissive parent of a teen who knocked up one of his classmates."

I know educators can easily add to this list:

I'm an excuse-making parent who believes everything my kid tells me.

My kid has a disability and I expect everyone to bend over backwards for her without expecting her to carry her load.

I'm a parent who expects that my unmotivated, irritating child will be passed in school without having to do anything to earn it.

When displays of disrespect that may or may not be purposely fanned by outside factors occur in school, we have to deal with it. A comprehensive approach to discipline requires that educators possess three sets of skills: crisis management, short-term strategies and long-term strategies. Crisis management is needed when a chair is being thrown or when students are fighting. Long-term strategies require that we understand what motivates children to exhibit challenging behaviors and that we do our share to prevent their occurrence. Short-term strategies require that we defuse potentially explosive moments such as that exhibited by Phil to Mr. Jones. While good discipline requires attention to all factors, this book highlights short-term strategies to use before a crisis occurs and gives some ideas about long-term strategies that are needed to prevent power struggles from developing.

IDENTIFYING THE PROBLEM

Power struggles develop when students refuse to follow the rules, fail to accept a consequence or they follow the rules and may even accept the consequences but with an "attitude." Some students are actively defiant and challenge authority at every turn while others are quietly hostile, like those who refuse to talk or do their work. Although those who are passive-aggressive can be frustrating to work with, the authority of the educator is most obviously challenged by students who are verbally and actively challenging. Not only is there a power struggle going on between the teacher and student, there is usually a classroom full of onlookers (students) who are watching every move. It is these moments in particular that we seek to defuse before things get out of hand.

Many teachers report the following forms of verbal defiance:

You can't make me!

You're not my mother!

SOOOOO!

No!

Why do we have to know that?

That's stupid.

This class sucks!!

My daddy says_____.

Examples of non-verbal active defiance are:

continuously coming in late

flicking a finger

smirking

throwing things

sitting slouched or with elbows folded

bothering others

Questions

1. Are there any other defiant behaviors you have experienced from students? Write these down.

2. Of the one(s) listed on the previous page, put a circle around those that you have experienced.

3. How do you feel when you are the victim of one or more of these responses?

4. Think of a student or situation involving difficult students that you find challenging.

5. How do you usually react to the situation?

6. How do you want to react to the situation?

Most educators feel angry when their buttons are pushed and they let their anger take hold by pushing back. While the "fight or flight" response makes that reaction understandable, it only serves to escalate the situation leading to a no-win outcome. Typically, the final move used by the teacher is to either isolate the student in time-out or send the student to the office. Rarely do either of these solutions work.

WHAT DOES WORK?

The three most common motivations that drive people to attack others are the needs for **respect, belonging** and **power.** Students often complain about peers and adults who disrespect them. Somebody who cuts us off on the highway shows little respect. We feel angry and hostile. Most of us keep our desire for revenge at the level of fantasy because we receive enough respect in other areas of our lives to compensate for those who show us little. Unfortunately, some act out that revenge.

All people need to feel important, and we feel important when others treat us with respect and dignity. Likewise, people need to feel bonded with others. The growth of gangs is but one manifestation of a society in which growing numbers of young people feel disconnected from the mainstream. Finally, we all need to know and believe that we can influence others and control what happens to us; a view that my ideas, behaviors or actions can actually affect things that happen. When one or more of these needs is not met, the stage is set for a child to resort to undesirable behavior, including direct challenges to the teacher.

We must remember that school is for all children, including those we find unattractive or hostile, those who misbehave and those who don't give their best. It is our professional duty to welcome and teach them with enthusiasm, care and courage. To do less diminishes ourselves and all of society. We offer some highly effective prevention and intervention strategies that educators can use to address these needs. Our goal is to understand how students are motivated to act in unacceptable, intrusive ways so that we can identify classroom strategies and persuasive skills to influence their behaviors.

PREVENTION STRATEGIES

1. CONVEY WARMTH

a. Greet students

Make it your practice to greet students. Say hello to each one every day when they are little and no less than twice a week when they are older. Welcome them as they arrive. An occasional "gimmicky" thing such as sending a greeting card may be appreciated.

b. Call by name

Learn their names early and use them often. Students are impressed when they feel known by their teacher. Further, it is much easier to command respect during disciplinary moments with students you know.

c. Keep attuned to their needs and interests

You can use interest inventories (see example on page 14). Ask students to regularly offer suggestions in a "suggestion box" about how the class can be more interesting or meaningful. Some teachers use the "index card" method by asking students to regularly write down what makes it hard for them to learn and what helps them learn.

d. Use the 2 x 10 method

Choose one of your students with whom you currently do considerable battle. Make a commitment to spend two uninterrupted, undivided minutes of your attention each day for ten consecutive days in an effort to build a different kind of relationship. You may ask any question, elicit the student's interests or share your own during this two-minute sequence. You may not correct the student or in any way use this time to persuade the student to change his behavior. After ten days, assess the relationship. Most teachers who use this method have found that initially they do about 90% of the initiating with the student. By the end of the tenth day, there is generally a 50-50 give and take.

e. Call student(s) at home

Think of one or two students you currently have who create problems in the classroom and who appear to be of relatively high status. Call at least one of them at home to discuss your concerns in an effort to find solutions. If a parent answers, respectfully ask to speak directly to the child.

2. GIVE OPPORTUNITIES FOR STUDENTS TO BE IN CHARGE

Students who push our buttons often have little real control in their lives. They act out to experience influence and gain attention. We can often work successfully with these students by addressing their control needs before problems arise.

Interest Inventory

*Name:*_____

Concerning this class, I am a person who...

likes_____

hates_____

can_____

cannot_____

would never _____

would rather _____

wants to learn how to_____

would be better off if_____

is really good at_____

gets angry when_____

"bugs" other people when_____

has the good habit of_____

has the bad habit of_____

wishes I could change the way I_____

wishes I could change the way other people_____

Outside of school, I am a person who...

never misses watching the TV show entitled_____

will someday _____

enjoys doing_____

a. Let them make some of the rules

People who lack real power and influence are much more likely to break the rules of others as a way of asserting their need for control. It works well to give students opportunities to make and/or revise classroom rules.

b. Give responsible jobs

Challenging students are often surprisingly responsible when they are given opportunities to be responsible. For example, a school in Baltimore has a "student ambassador" program in which students who have moved are eligible to become school ambassadors. The job of an ambassador is to welcome new students to the school who have recently moved, give them a tour and share such things as rules and procedures. Some of the most difficult students in the school make the best student ambassadors. An ambassador is expected to display a high standard of performance and behavior in order to maintain that status. All classes, particularly at an elementary level, have many functions that can be performed by students: passing out papers, inspecting bathrooms, giving directions, greeting visitors when they come into the room, etc.

Think about your classroom and all of the things that have to be done for things to run smoothly. Which of these functions can you assign to your students? Identify one or more of these functions that you can give to a challenging student.

c. Put them in charge of pets or people

Students who seem to care little about others (those with low empathy) need opportunities to positively bond with others. For some, this can be achieved by creating situations in which they learn that they can make a positive difference in the lives of other living things. Caring for pets, being a big brother or sister for a younger child with problems or partnering with senior citizens in need at a nursing home are but a few specific ways of moving towards a desirable outcome. Since many of these students have a history of being verbally, sexually or physically abused by others, they need to be supervised while participating in these kinds of activities.

d. One-week positivity campaign

Challenging students make themselves hard to like. It is as if they practice inventing new ways to turn people off. It is necessary for educators to become tougher at refusing to reject them than they are at triggering rejection. Spend one day observing a student who really irritates you. Work hard to find some redeeming positive quality that you might build on. For the next week, be certain to affirm this positive quality at least once each day.

e. Defer to their opinion

This can be a powerful way of affirming a challenging student. Model respect to all students by deferring to the opinion of a difficult one. If a student asks a question about something, say, "Go ask Sally about that. She's good at_____." When students hear their teacher respond with respect, they are more apt to respond in kind.

3. BE RESPECTFUL OF DIFFERENCES IN THE WAYS STUDENTS LEARN

Schools are for teaching and learning. The latest research finds that there are at least seven distinct intelligences with only two being emphasized in school. The two that receive the greatest emphasis are verbal/linguistic and logical/mathematical. It may be that a preponderance of behavior problems comes from students whose strengths lie mainly in one or more of the remaining intelligences. Researchers such as Howard Gardner and Thomas Armstrong suggest the importance of meaningfully delivering curriculum in diverse ways. While interviewing students, John Goodlad found that activities which they experience as motivational in school are:

1. interviewing people
2. taking field trips
3. acting things out
4. building or drawing things
5. making collections
6. carrying out independent projects

Suggestion: While reviewing your lessons plan(s), think about specific ways that each of these types of activities can be included on a daily basis within your classroom.

Wanda Lincoln (*Instruction Influences Student Discipline*) developed a checklist that illustrates the connection between instruction and student discipline.

Instruction Influences Student Discipline

Below is a list of teacher behaviors that are often mentioned as contributing to classroom discipline problems. In other words, if the lesson is not taught well, students will "let the teacher know!" If you agree, this may serve as a checklist to do a self-evaluation. Or you may want to discuss these with colleagues and do some peer observations.

1. The teacher sits at the desk most of the time, not moving or mingling with the students.

2. The teacher has an unenthusiastic, low or uninteresting voice.

3. The teacher is easily sidetracked by one student's irrelevant question.

4. The teacher is tied solely to the textbook and ignores students' interests.

5. The teacher repeats the student's answers too frequently.

6. Concepts are left before they have been clarified and/or independent work expected before understanding has been checked.

7. Questions are poorly worded, clouding discussion.

8. When a student asks a question, only the teacher is expected to answer.

9. The teacher neglects to tie the content or materials to the prior knowledge of the students.

10. Too much time is given to teaching the lesson, and not enough focus is on what is being learned!

11. The teacher does not prepare materials before the lesson, leaving "down time" for the students to FILL!

What would you add?

_____

_____

_____

_____

_____

_____

Questions and suggestions that help prevent power struggles in the classroom:

1. When you visit someone in their home, what are some things they do that help you feel welcome?

2. What are some practices that others do that help you feel welcome in their home which you could apply in your classroom?

3. What teacher(s) did you have when you were in school that made you feel special or important? What did they do that gave you that feeling?

4. Identify at least three practices that you can do without changing your basic style of teaching that could promote a sense of connection with your students in the classroom.

5. Visit at least three other teachers in your school while they are teaching. Identify practices that you see them using that you consider to be good ways of building warmth.

6. What responsible jobs can you assign to your students to give them a sense of importance within the classroom?

7. What values do you believe are necessary for good learning and teaching to occur (i.e., respect, courteous listening, absence of verbal harassment)?

8. After you identify these values, invite your students to develop or modify classroom rules that reflect each of these values.

9. What realistic activities or experiences

involving people or pets can you generate for your students who are low in empathy so that they can relearn how to care for others?

10. When teaching each lesson, can you make the goals of the lesson clear to yourself and your students? A common challenge of students is to ask "why" they need to learn what is being taught. Aside from the fact that it might be on the test, work to help them understand how the learning is likely to provide benefits.

INTERVENTION STRATEGIES

While prevention practices are usually effective, some students persist in challenging authority. Their needs are too strong to be managed by prevention strategies alone. When students present challenging, button-pushing behaviors, we must respond with dignity to them while preserving our own. We must remind ourselves that we are the professional adult. Just as a doctor wouldn't yell at a patient who is bleeding all over him, we need to maintain our professionalism in the midst of crisis. At the same time, it is our duty to keep a student's offensive behavior from dominating the class.

Effective intervention strategies stop problem behavior while maintaining everybody's dignity.

Learn to stay personal without personalizing the student's hostile behavior

In his pioneering work with troubled youth, Fritz Redl spoke about the importance of adults being able to manage their "counteraggressive" impulses towards hostile children. It is important to recognize that troubled students will make you mad. They will get to you because they are experienced in getting people to dislike them. Permit yourself to honestly and privately express these frustrations. You will need to take good emotional care of yourself in order to hang in there. You also will need to take periodic vacations from such students. Develop a support network with colleagues that enables you to separate yourself from the student for brief periods. Let the student know that you are at least as stubborn as he or she is with an approach that says, "I know the game. You want to do everything you can to push me away because then you'll prove yet again that everybody and everything is unfair. But I'm not going away. I know you've got worth even though you don't think so."

The major key in working with button-pushing youngsters is staying personally involved with them while finding ways of refusing to take personally their obnoxious, irritating or threatening behaviors. There are four primary ways to accomplish this: take good emotional care of yourself, understand the hostility cycle, substitute less powerful words and images for those that usually trigger anger. Finally, learn and use defusing strategies.

Take good emotional care of yourself

There are many ways of doing this.

1. Develop a support network

Work out arrangements with colleagues that allow you to take brief breaks from students who are irritating. For example, you can work out a system in which you and a colleague or colleagues use each other. A green pass might signal that you just sent the student out for a break (there was no real errand to run). A yellow pass might ask for two or three minutes of time-out, while a purple pass might ask your colleague to keep the student as long as possible.

2. Counting forwards or backwards to 10 or more

3. Doing guided visualizations

Use relaxing images such as a walk in the woods, listening to ocean waves, taking a magical trip, being in the mountains. The more you allow yourself to get all senses involved (i.e., see the ocean, hear the waves, smell the sea, etc.), the more likely it is that the visualization will be effective.

4. Deep Breathing

Before reacting to a hostile word or image, take three or four deep breaths.

5. Listen to relaxing music

6. Make yourself laugh

A teacher I know imagines that when one of her students uses foul language, he does so with a bonnet in his hair and a pacifier in his mouth. The image makes her laugh and enables her to usually defuse the potentially explosive situation.

Questions

1. **Identify methods that you can use to keep yourself calm.**

   Maintaining self-control can be assisted through methods of relaxation. From the list provided, which strategies might best work for you?

2. **Can you think of other strategies that you currently use for relaxation or fun?**

   Of these, which can you do regularly?

Carving a daily niche for relaxation and fun should be a requirement when working with challenging people.

UNDERSTAND THE HOSTILITY CYCLE

A few years ago, I was working with a juvenile delinquent youth. It was our first meeting. Midway through the session, I felt a warm sensation on my face. Reaching up to feel further, it became immediately clear that Raoul had spit in my face. Watching him smirk at me with challenge at hand, I remembered the "hostility cycle" which I had learned years earlier but desperately needed at that moment. Children who view the world in a hostile way provoke hostility in others. When that gets them the hostility they are looking for, it provides their latest evidence that the world is a hostile place (*figure one* shows this phenomenon).

The only way to break through the cycle is for adults who are "regulars" in the lives of the student to refuse feeding into the cycle. With spit on my face, I glared at Raoul and assertively said, "Do you have a tissue?!" Perhaps owing to the unexpectedness of this response, Raoul appeared to be caught off guard. He hesitantly said, "No, I ain't got no tissues." I nodded at him, got out of

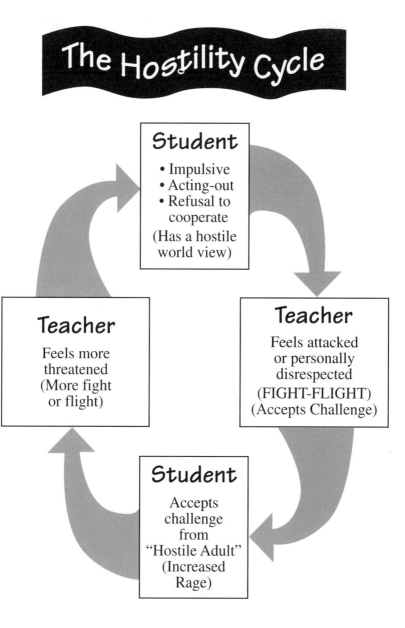

(Figure One)

my seat, got a few tissues, removed my eyeglasses and wiped my face. Afterward, I said,

> "Raoul, you and I are new to each other and we are stuck with each other. The State says that you and I need to meet in order for you to qualify to leave this place. Now in the future, I'm sure there'll be times that we won't like each other very much. If you ever say anything to me that pisses me off, I guarantee that I'll never spit in your face because if I did spit I'd be showing no respect for you or me. I'll also expect that if you ever get mad at me, you'll find another way. Even though I don't know much about you, I've got to believe that you have too much respect for yourself or others who may care about you to show that kind of disrespect. Do I make myself clear?"

To my relief, Raoul stopped. By understanding the hostility cycle, we can give ourselves a choice to react in another way.

Suggestion: Important additional information on this topic can be found in the work of Wood and Long (1991) Life Space Intervention.

Questions

1. What do students do that trigger hostility in you?

2. Why do you think they do these things?

3. Using the hostility cycle graph (page 29), think of one student with whom you often have power struggles. Write down what the student says or does that triggers you. Write down how you usually respond. Write down how the student responds to your response. Can you see how the hostility cycle is at the root of power struggles? You will shortly learn lots of new ways to handle these triggers.

SUBSTITUTE LESS POWERFUL WORDS AND IMAGES FOR THOSE THAT ARE DISTURBING

A wise colleague once gave me advice that has stayed with me throughout my career and generally served me well in working with troubled youth. He told me that any student who is giving it bad to an educator is getting it at least as bad or worse from some important source in his life. My colleague shared his belief that rarely as educators do we know exactly where the kid's misery is coming from, but no doubt it's there. He told me it is important to keep this in mind because challenging students make themselves so resentful that it is hard to see them as anything other than a hated object.

At that time there was a student in my class who fit this description to a tee. My colleague suggested that if I could learn to hear and see **less** threatening images generated by this student, I would have a much better chance of responding effectively to his "button-pushing" behaviors. The student often used offensive language and gestures. My colleague asked me how I might respond to this student if he called me a "chair" instead of an "s.o.b." How might I react, he asked, if I imagined a friendly wave from the student instead of his middle finger flicked high in the air. Finally, he told me that it is important to be forgiving of both the student for triggering anger and of myself for losing my cool. I began to see his point but it wasn't easy. As we've seen, all people are human and have their buttons. While an occasional lapse is understandable and should be greeted with forgiveness, the real key was that I needed to change my reaction to the student's provocation. I might not be able to change the student's behavior, but I could certainly change my reaction.

When we provide new pictures or words to difficult situations, we are performing a technique that is called "reframing." It can be a very powerful way of regaining a sense of personal control so that we can go back to the drawing board and begin to rethink ways of best reaching a challenging student.

Power struggles can often be either prevented or reduced through reframing. If we view a driver on the highway who cuts us off as an "inconsiderate, dangerous slob," chances are very good that we will feel frustration and anger. But if we discover that the driver was racing to the hospital after learning of a serious accident to his child, we view the same behavior with understanding and compassion. In an objective sense, there is no excuse for behaviors that endanger others. But how we choose to experience the incident through the words and images we create powerfully influences our reactions.

Let's look at some ways of doing this with typical discipline problems.

1. Late to class

Most teachers get upset with students who are late. And getting to class on time is certainly desirable and should be encouraged. However, the good news is that the student came. Reframing requires that we see coming late as preferable to not coming at all. A reframing statement is, "Bill, I'm disappointed that you are again late. But coming late is better than not being here at

all. It must have taken effort to get here."
Reframing requires conveying the attitude
to the student that he or she is more
important than his behavior. You can set
a limit by expressing disappointment and
even by implementing a consequence (i.e.,
requiring the student to stay late), but the

emphasis in reframing is highlighting the person's benefits (no matter how minimal) rather than the specific outcome.

Suggestion: Most educators will need to practice doing a reframing several times before they are ready to convey the message with genuineness and without sarcasm. Rehearse and role-play in private and implement only when able to do so without sarcasm.

Let's look at some other possible problems and how they can be "reframed":

2. Temper tantrum

The good news is that nobody got hurt. "Sally, do you know that when you got really mad this morning, you showed really good self-control. Even though you knocked over a chair and used words that are against the rules, you didn't hurt anyone. That was good. Let's look at how you might do an even better job next time you get mad."

Suggestion: Remember, you can and will often choose to implement a consequence. It is the degree of emphasis that is important. Successfully implementing this approach requires an attitude from the educator that says, "You (student) are more important than what you do, although poor choices usually have consequences."

3. Excessive talking to others

The good news is that this child is socially connected. His presence also gives others an opportunity to learn how to work with distractions present. "Ben, I'd love if you could remind yourself not to talk out of turn. But when you do, it reminds us that getting our work done is necessary even when there are distractions present."

Questions

1. What behaviors occur in your classroom that you find objectionable?

2. Which students show these behaviors regularly?

3. Think of any positive benefits either to you or the class when the students show these undesirable behaviors (i.e., if a student does no homework, there is one less paper to grade which means more time to give to those who turned in their work. In a sense, the student has donated her time to her classmates).

4. Imagine the student is in front of you and try to express these benefits genuinely.

5. Repeat the process until your words and beliefs are compatible (this often takes a long time because we are unaccustomed to noticing positive aspects of behaviors we find objectionable).

ACTIVITY FOR REFRAMING

The concept: "People accommodate change more readily when they do not feel forced to let go of the familiar."

1. Identify a chronically irritating student.

2. Identify the problem behavior.

3. Identify positive aspects and benefits of the student's behavior. Relatively speaking, what is acceptable about the student's behavior? How do you, the class or, lastly, the student benefit?

4. Imagine the student is in front of you and try to express these benefits genuinely. You may also express your displeasure and/or give a consequence, but you must highlight the benefits.

5. Implement the strategy with a student

who shows excessive inappropriate behavior even after more conventional strategies have been tried.

LEARN AND USE DEFUSING STRATEGIES

When a student or students are behaving in a way that interrupts the teaching/learning process, action needs to be taken which effectively ends the problem moment. Defusing increases the likelihood that you can end the problem moment while still being in control. In this section, we look at the goals of defusing, basic defusing skills, specific statements to use that help in defusing, additional steps that may be necessary, dealing with the rest of the class and follow-up with student.

Goals of Defusing

There are four goals that are very helpful to achieve when defusing a power struggle:

a. Dignity for the student

We are least likely to feel like wanting to

extend dignity to students when they behave unacceptably. It is important, however, to keep in mind that dignity is easy to do when students are nice. A true professional educator responds with disapproval *and* dignity to displays of misbehavior. We believe that part of our job is to treat all students with dignity and respect. To do less invites hostility and retaliation. Keep in mind: All students in your class have tenure. If they leave feeling humiliated, they'll be back to get even tomorrow!

b. Dignity for yourself

It is equally important that we preserve our own dignity when under attack. The teacher must be able to assertively stand up so that she is not viewed as milquetoast. The key, when your button is being pushed, is to locate a response that enables you to stand up without fighting back.

c. Keep the student in class

There are times when a student is so out of line that it becomes impossible to teach or for other students to learn. At these times, a trip to the principal for "time-out" may be appropriate. However, it is best whenever possible to end the conflict while keeping the student in the classroom. Frequent referrals elsewhere for discipline diminish the adult's authority. It signals that the adult-in-charge is unable to handle a difficult situation. Worse, it does nothing to show a realistic solution to a challenging interpersonal problem that can be applied by the students who witness the incident. For example, no student is able to order another to the principal's office!

d. Teach an alternative to aggression

How we respond to conflict is a critical element in either gaining or losing credibility with our students when we wish to teach them skills that they can use. With many schools establishing peer mediation and conflict-resolution programs for students, we believe that it is necessary for adults-in-charge to model the very strategies that they are wanting students to learn. When a student pushes a teacher's button, the incident actually provides the teacher with an opportunity to show students how to stand up effectively to conflict without either caving in or fighting back. These moments provide important reinforcement of conflict-resolution programs because students see an important adult using a skill that the school is promoting for students.

BASIC DEFUSING SKILLS

a. P.E.P.

Before things careen out of control, most potentially difficult power struggles can successfully be solved by the educator giving his corrective message to the student with privacy, eye-contact and proximity (P.E.P.). Successful use of P.E.P. requires that the teacher frequently "cruise" while teaching so that he is in close natural proximity with all students throughout the day. This makes it possible to blend corrective messages with those that are appreciative. When all students know that a regular part of the teacher's behavior is making frequent private contact with each student for purposes of giving feedback, it is rare that student defensiveness occurs when being corrected. Remember, a big reason for power struggles is the student's desire to seek status among his peers, and drawing the teacher into public battles is a favored method for achieving status (Note: do not insist upon eye contact with those students who won't look).

b. Non-verbal P.E.P.

The use of index cards and post-it notes provides a nice alternative to verbal forms of P.E.P. Index cards or post-it notes should have words or phrases on them which convey either corrective or appreciative statements. Separate cards or notes can say such things as: "thanks," "way to go," "please chill," "stop." Cards or notes can also use pictures or colors such as a stop sign, green or red light. Sayings with pictures can easily be created as illustrated on page 43.

c. L.A.A.D.

When a student is more agitated or challenging, L.A.A.D. is suggested. This acronym stands for Listening, Acknowledging, Agreeing, Deferring. Skillful use of one or more of these components is 90% effective in defusing a power struggle.

Let's take a typical situation that can easily blow up to show how these skills can be used. After making a request, Luis loudly tells his teacher, "you can't make me." A power struggle is likely if the teacher accepts the challenge: (i.e., "yes I can," "I'll call home," "that is no way to talk to me, get out!"). L.A.A.D. provides a sound alternative:

Listening

"You must be upset Luis and right now you are in no mood to listen. I'll respect that." Listening requires that the person receiving the message hears either the content or the mood of the speaker and feeds that understanding back to the speaker.

Acknowledging

"Luis, if I understand you correctly, you are telling me that you are not planning to do what is asked. Did I get that right?... Thanks for letting me know your plan." Acknowledging can be done with words or actions. A knowing look can serve the same purpose. Attention is best redirected to the lesson at hand.

Agreeing

"Luis, you are right about that. I cannot make you do things. The real question is whether you can make yourself do it, and then will you feel proud. Good luck." Agreeing is very powerful because it acknowledges the real control had by the student and puts the responsibility right back where it belongs.

Deferring

"Luis, I have no idea why you would say that right in front of the whole class and I'm embarrassed. Let's talk after class to avoid a fight." Even when the student doesn't stay after class, offering an option to continue exploring the student's concern(s) at a time when it is possible to provide adequate attention is often effective in defusing a continuation of the power struggle.

Activity for you to try:

Write down things that students say or do which trigger anger in you and make you want to fight back. Unfortunately, some common examples are:

"SOOO"

"NO!"

"You're not my mother!"

"I don't have to."

"This class is boring."

"This class sucks!"

"Why do we have to do _____."

"Whatever."

Are there any others that you experience?
Are there any non-verbal behaviors that students
do which seem designed to push your button?
Add any additional verbal or non-verbal behaviors
to this list.

_____

_____

Imagine a student is now doing one of the
above behaviors. Using the L.A.A.D. paradigm,
practice writing and then saying a statement or
statements in each category.

A. Problem behavior that pushes my button

_____

_____

B. Strategies

1. Listening _____

2. Acknowledging _____

3. Agreeing _____

4. Deferring _____

SPECIFIC DEFUSING STATEMENTS

There are many additional statements that may be helpful in defusing specific problem situations. The key is to maintain the correct attitude we discussed earlier: **stay personal with the student without personalizing the problem behavior and then stand up without fighting back.** It is the presence of this attitude guided by the goals of defusing that opens the door to many possible words, sentences and actions which can end a power struggle. Choosing the words is a matter of seeing what closely fits your way right now and/or practicing how you'd like to be. Several additional statements are offered for your analysis. We encourage you to try on any or all of them after imagining a button-pushing incident has occurred. Actually say them aloud. Read them several times to gain familiarity. See which ones most closely represent who you are and then modify to give them your own flavor. Remember, the words work when conveyed with the right attitude.

Defusing Statements That Avoid Power Struggles:

a. I'm disappointed that you are choosing to use such angry words even though I'm sure there is much to be upset about.

b. I am really concerned! It is very important that I understand why you are so mad. Please tell me later when I can really listen.

c. Your words (actions) tell me you are bored. It takes a lot of discipline to hang in there when you are unsure about why we are doing certain things. Thanks for hanging in there.

d. I know you are angry but there is no problem too big that can't be solved. Let's use words to solve the problem.

e. You're just not yourself today and that must feel lousy.

f. We both know there are other ways of telling how we feel while still being respectful. I look forward to hearing from you after class.

g. Throwing chairs doesn't make problems go away. It only creates new ones. Let's use our words to say why we feel so mad!

h. I really want to understand what I did to annoy you. But swearing at me doesn't help. Let's talk later when we can be alone.

i. Wow, you must be feeling awfully mad to use those words in front of everyone.

j. Wow, you must be mad to embarrass me like this in front of everyone. It makes me want to fight back, but then we'd never solve the problem. Later is the time to handle this.

k. I'm glad you trust me enough to tell me how you feel and I'm concerned. Any suggestions for improvement are appreciated. Please leave them in the "suggestion box."

l. There may be some truth to what you are saying but it is hard for me to really hear you when you use words which are disrespectful.

m. That is an interesting opinion. Tell me more after class.

n. When did you start (feeling, thinking, believing) that? Tell me after class.

Practice defusing statements

1. Write down a button-pushing behavior that you experience from a student.

2. Picture the student being right in front of you.

3. Pick one of the defusing statements and say it while trying to use a tone of voice that conveys **firmness and respect.**

4. Practice that statement at least five times.

5. Pick another if that one doesn't seem to fit and repeat.

6. Continue as needed.

ADDITIONAL STEPS THAT MAY BE NECESSARY

Our research and observations found that a certain sequence can be followed which virtually eliminates potential power struggles. The sequence with a brief explanation of each step follows:

1. **State the rule and consequence using P.E.P.**

   Student and teacher dignity are most apt to be preserved when a rule, direction, corrective comment or consequence is given with privacy, eye contact (when possible) and proximity.

2. **Ignore the last hook**

   It is not unusual for the corrected student to

grunt, grumble or loudly whisper after the P.E.P. moment. In most cases, it is the student's last hurrah! It is his or her need to have the last word to save face. If the student's problem behavior stops after the grunt, you are best served by ignoring the hook. For example, the educator is well advised to ignore a student's "whatever" when it is followed quickly with compliance.

3. Use listening or acknowledging

Most students let go of their need for control when they are affirmed by the teacher. Active listening at the content and/or feelings level is often very effective.

4. Use agreeing and defer

If a student continues the battle after you have "listened and acknowledged" this step can be very powerful. For example, a student says, "My daddy says I don't have to!" A combined agreeing and defer would be, "then that puts you in a tough spot. I wouldn't want to disobey my father and neither do you. We'll talk later when we can figure out a good solution."

(Note: It is usually good practice to offer to call the student's parent(s) in the deferring

*session you have with the student. Most
students are quick to retract their parent's
condoning behavior when confronted in
that way.)*

5. Tell there's a power struggle happening

Most students who have continued to this point,
will stop when you acknowledge that a fight is
about to break out. "Sue, I see it one way and
you see it differently. I can feel myself about
to fight with you and I know that neither of us
likes to lose. We'll talk more later."

6. Offer the door

When a student's behavior persists at interrup-
ting the teaching/learning process, it may be
time for a temporary time-out either within the
classroom (for younger students), to a planning
room, or to the office. The student is essentially
offered a last chance: "Sue, I need this to stop
right now or for you to leave. I hope you
choose to stay (very important to share this)
but I'll understand if you need to go. If you
go, come back when you're ready."

7. Give temporary control

If the student continues, there is no help
available and the student is making it

impossible to continue teaching, you can usually regain control by letting it go temporarily. The teacher would approach the student, hand over a piece of chalk and say, "Sue, I can't continue. Why don't you teach for the next few minutes. You're in charge. Anything goes except class dismissed!" The teacher may choose to sit in the student's seat and do some role reversal. When you sense that the student is running out of steam, get up, go over to the student, take the chalk and continue on with the lesson.

8. Decide if a consequence is necessary

If any of the above actions succeed in ending the problem moment, you still need to decide on a consequence. A consequence should be given if you can see how the problem student will learn from it or it should be given if you feel you must take some visible action for purposes of showing all of the other students that following the rules is important. In the event that a decision is made to give a consequence so that visibility is shown to others, it must be done in a dignified way. For example, after class the teacher meets Sue and says, "Sue, I'm sure glad we were able to stop our argument. I appreciate that. But I want you to remember to follow the rules, and it is important that other students realize that mistakes need to be fixed." The educator can then give the consequence or develop a consequence with the student.

Consequences work best when done privately. All students may know that a consequence has been or will be given but they do not need to know what it is or hear it expressed.

Review: Steps for when rules are broken

1. State the rule and consequence using P.E.P.

2. Ignore the hook

3. Use listening and acknowledging

4. Use agreeing and deferring

5. Tell there's a power struggle happening

6. Offer the door but invite to stay

7. Give temporary control

8. Decide if a consequence is necessary

THE PRIVATE THREE-STEP TECHNIQUE

When a student persists in doing the behaviors

that we've been discussing, the "private three-step" is a very effective method that can be done privately. When alone with the student, the educator uses three statements which are conveyed in a respectful and assertive manner. Let's suppose that Lee has been verbally offensive several times. The three-step works as follows:

1. Use an "I-Message"

"Lee, when you use those words in class, I get upset, disappointed and even embarrassed."

2. Use the "what have I done"

"We have a problem. What have I done to you to deserve the way you've been treating me in class." (Note: This must be delivered as a genuine question, with no sarcasm or attempt to elicit guilt. Another way to make this work is to say "I must have done something to make you feel so upset. Please tell me what it is.")

3. Use the "problem solving"

"If we have a problem, then we need to work it out."

Suggested private three-step activity

1. Think of a student who regularly does something that bothers you

2. Identify a time that you can be alone with the student

3. Use the three-step

    a. I-Message - "When you do _____, I feel _____."

    b. "We have a problem. What have I done to you to deserve the way you've been treating me in class." Or, "I must have done something to make you feel so upset. Please tell me what it is."

c. "If we have a problem, then we need to work it out."

It is important that these words are spoken slowly, with good eye contact (unless the student won't offer it due to either cultural or emotional reasons), and in a firm yet respectful manner.

DEALING WITH THE REST OF THE CLASS

Sustaining most power struggles is concern that other students will begin to behave in the same way as the problem student unless the teacher takes decisive action. And there is certainly an element of truth to this concern. Unfortunately, this concern too often leads to an escalating, "get-tough" response, which fans the flames. As the professional, it is absolutely essential that the educator refrain from falling prey to this phenomenon. It is usually necessary to "stop and think" before acting. We are continuously trying to promote this to students, and it is therefore necessary that we model it. The old-fashioned suggestion of "walk the talk" is particularly relevant here. The teacher must stand up to the assault without fighting back. She must present herself as capable of stopping the problem while preserving the dignity of the student and herself. Accomplishing these goals is achievable in most cases. Use of the defusing strategies shared earlier is one approach. Another is to deal effectively with the rest of the class. To do so, the teacher is encouraged to be honest with his/her students.

Immediately after a challenging incident has occurred, it is common for other students either verbally or non-verbally to wonder "what are you going to do about it?" In response to this reality, the teacher is encouraged to anticipate by saying something like,

"I know you all just heard what LeShon said and I'll bet most of you are wondering what I am going to do about it. So I'm going to be up front with all of you. The answer is that I have no idea what I'm going to do about it because I have no idea why LeShon is so upset today that he needs to use language that all of us, including LeShon, knows is inappropriate. So until I can find out what's bothering him, I'll have to say that I'm not sure. But would any of you like to know what I'd like to do if I could?.....I wish I could be alone with LeShon to find out, or I wish I could be at the beach right now relaxing. But I won't be able to do either, because my job is to teach you right now. So let's open our books and get going.

The combination of honesty and, if possible, humor can often help to defuse the situation and "buy" time until a more thoughtful solution can be found. When a challenging student stops challenging after the teacher gives a response, it may still be necessary to give a consequence to the student. If LeShon settled down during class following the teacher's response, the teacher may still choose to implement a consequence as a way of either following school procedure or to make a statement to LeShon and others. Most important, however, is what is emphasized. For example, LeShon is told in private, "LeShon, I feel pleased that after you got upset, you settled down. I'm glad we were able to work it out. As you know, swearing is against the rules, and I'm also a bit concerned that others may get the idea that such language is okay in class. So I will be submitting a referral and there will probably be consequences. But I am pleased that we were able to work things out. I hope you have a better remainder of the day." We have found that approximately 90% of all students respond very positively to this type of intervention.

There are three primary purposes sought by students who challenge authority regularly: they are attempting to have influence in their lives;

they are protesting oppressive limits imposed by others; they have little if any direction or structure and are looking for boundaries.

Effective discipline in a group situation focuses on prevention. Show challenging students that they have influence by welcoming them and asking for their opinion. Invite them to join in developing classroom rules. Expect them to behave and hold them accountable when they don't.

In summary, concern for the rest of the class can be met by:

1. Defusing the power struggle by using one of the methods suggested earlier. (see pages 48-50)

2. Acknowledging that a challenge occurred (i.e., "most of you probably heard or saw what was said or done").

3. Safeguarding your and the challenging student's dignity (i.e., "and you're probably wondering what I'm going to do about it. In all honesty, I need to first find out why the student is so upset that he's doing something that is against the rules.")

4. Using humor (when possible) (i.e., "How many of you would like to know what I

would like to do right now if I could? I'd like to _____.")

5. Redirecting class attention to the lesson (i.e., "but I won't be able to do that because I'm here right now and my job is to teach today's lesson. So let's open our books and get busy.")

6. Reminding yourself to include practices of prevention.

Follow-up with the student

It is extraordinarily important that we refuse to give up on difficult students. A bad day needs to be followed by a welcoming attitude on the part of the teacher. We cannot afford to lose the student. If he's expelled to the mall and creates problems there, we haven't done much to make him more responsible and we haven't done a thing to make the world a safer place. It can be helpful to remember the saying: "all students have tenure." Say something like, "Bob, we had a rough day yesterday. It was tough for both of us. Welcome back today. I know it's going to be better."

If you, the educator, exploded at the student in front of the class and probably contributed to embarrassment, this is a perfect time to offer an apology. You also get an opportunity to show all of the other students in the class how "remorse" feels and how to express empathy. Say, "Bob, your behavior made me mad and I think I'm owed an apology. But whether or not you apologize, it didn't make it right for me to go off on you and embarrass you in front of the class. My apologies. Welcome back!"

POWER STRUGGLE SCENARIOS

Now it is your turn to practice using prevention and intervention strategies. Read the problem situations below and decide what type of prevention and intervention strategies you would use. You might prefer working collaboratively with colleagues on these scenarios while including role-playing, discussion and brainstorming.

1. Nancy is working and her teacher begins to pass out papers to other students. She gets agitated for no apparent reason and exclaims, "This class is stupid!!"

2. A teacher asks a child to stop running in the hall. The student responds, "You can't make me, fatso!"

3. Bill raises his hand to answer a question in class. His teacher calls on another

student. Bill slams his hand down on his desk and yells, "I'm done raising my hand, you never call on me."

4. Ann continually blurts out answers without raising her hand.

5. George regularly leaves his seat to visit others during work time.

6. Lafonso refuses to work in a cooperative group.

7. Horace makes faces at other students to annoy them during class discussion.

AN ARTICLE FOR THOUGHT

The article you are about to read appeared in the journal *Reclaiming Children and Youth*, Spring, 1995. It will provide a summary of important concepts and strategies along with a few more ideas.

Classroom Counteraggression

I recently met a preschool teacher who told me about a four-year-old child who constantly uses guns in play. He drew guns, built guns with Legos, and talked about guns. Her efforts to prohibit such play were met with even more intense aggressive play. She was understandably concerned that other children would become aggressive, and she was trying to promote an atmosphere of cooperation and nonviolence.

When I asked her if she knew much about this child's background with guns, she dejectedly told me that Deacon had seen his cousin killed and that his uncle was the recent victim of a drive-by shooting that took place in his home. Deacon was in the next room when this happened. It was clear from the discussion that this young child was stressed, frightened, and preoccupied with these events and was reliving some or all of this through his play. In effect, he had no other place to turn to for safety and meaning than to his play.

His teacher needed help in seeing that to give this child a sense of control; she needed to find ways of engaging his need for guns within his play. She was encouraged to do a lot of "active listening" by following the themes that he was setting. He needed to be engaged by someone who cared and was able to decode the message. He needed to know that she would do everything she could to make sure he felt safe in the classroom. Eventually, his preoccupation diminished at least temporarily, though the absence of a strong emotional support network made his eventual outcome far from certain.

With so many children experiencing major crises on an almost daily basis, we must reframe our concept of the classroom to include affirmation and validation of their real-life experiences. Since wounded students who externalize their pain often project it onto those who are closest, we need to be prepared for their expressions of anger, torment, frustration, and humiliation. While Deacon confined his aggression to gunplay in the classroom, many other students target fellow students or adults.

It is easy and natural to either fight or run when under attack. Making a difference with such students requires that we do neither. The needed response is for us to stand up without fighting back. It is to let the student know that we find his or her behavior objectionable, but that we are able to push beyond it while, at the same time, preserving our dignity and the integrity of a classroom full of shocked, wondering students.

The major challenge when students elicit feelings of counter-aggression within us is to find ways of staying personally involved with them without personalizing their misery. We must realize that students who attack are virtually always under attack. If attacked back, the never-ending cycle perpetuates itself. Since such students see the world as a hostile place, they often set others up to reject them so that their world view is confirmed. When we continue to care and refuse to give up, it is common for them to push harder and harder until finally they surrender to the possibility of bonding. Continuing to care is no easy process, but it is wonderfully rewarding at the end of the road.

I recall Jimmy, seven years old when I first met him, who was a handful in his second-grade classroom. Frequently out of his seat, aggressive with others, and easily angered, Jimmy's patient, capable teacher often sought support. A network of support staff in collaboration with her efforts helped Jimmy get through that year and the next few. I lost contact with him for a few years, but I met him again when he was in seventh grade. By that time, Jimmy was even more troubled and troubling. All of his teachers knew him as a troublemaker by the second week of school. When I asked him if there was anything at all positive about school, he eventually told me that he "kinda" liked his English teacher. As I asked for details, Jimmy said, "She understands kids, and she lets us tell it like it is." Somewhat guardedly, he next told me that because of her he was becoming "a poet." At my request, Jimmy brought a stack of poems into my office the following day. Most of them were written on torn paper and used napkins. I could not put them

down; they revealed the inner workings of this troubled boy.
One of his poems said:

> I feel like stone
>
> Solid and cold
>
> As the bread that is so old,
>
> Like ice which hurts to the touch
>
> It fills my heart with pain too much
>
> Where is the comfort I need to survive
>
> Where is the hope to keep me alive

I couldn't help but realize that this student who was negative, nasty, defiant, and rebellious had such depth of feeling. Working effectively with such students requires that we look beyond the obvious and respond. The hope for this boy was in his teachers; and now, years later, Jimmy is in college studying to be one! In his words, he is making it because some of his teachers "refused to give up on me despite my best efforts to get them to throw in the towel!"

It is important to recognize that troubled students will make you mad. They will get to you because they are experienced in getting people to dislike them. Permit yourself to honestly and privately express these frustrations. You will need to take good emotional care of yourself in order to hang in there. You also will need to take periodic vacations from such students. Develop a support network with colleagues that enables you to separate the student from you for brief periods. Let the student know that you are at least as stubborn as he or she is with an approach that says "I know the game. You want to do everything you can to push me away, because then you'll prove yet again that everybody and everything are unfair. But I'm not going away. I know you've got worth even though you don't think so."

It also is necessary to be prepared for power struggles. They will test your resolve by trying to embarrass you in the classroom. It requires great courage and much skill to stand up and not fight back. Most problem moments can be defused through a combination of listening, acknowledging the student's concern, agreeing that there may be some truth in the student's accusation, and deferring to a private time for continued discussion.

Finally, it is very important that we not castigate ourselves when we occasionally do lose our cool. Like a champion prizefighter, success requires endurance and the strength to suffer an occasional knockdown.

In my work with juvenile delinquent youth, I often have noted that their most prized possession is a teddy bear. It was at first shocking and saddening to watch teenage boys asleep behind a locked door, clutching their teddy bear in a near-fetal position. These tough kids are emotional infants! They need nurturing *and* limit-setting.

BIBLIOGRAPHY OF TITLES RELATED TO DISCIPLINE WITH DIGNITY

Curwin, R. and Mendler, A. *Discipline with Dignity.* Alexandria, VA: Association for Curriculum Development, 1988

Curwin, R. *Rediscovering Hope.* Bloomington, IN: National Educational Service, 1992

Curwin, R. *Developing Responsibility and Self-Discipline.* Santa Cruz, CA: ETR Associates, 1990

Curwin, R. and Mendler, A. *Am I In Trouble?* Santa Cruz, CA: ETR Associates, 1990

Mendler, A. *Smiling at Yourself.* Santa Cruz, CA: ETR Associates, 1990

Mendler, A. *What Do I Do When?.........How To Achieve Discipline with Dignity in the Classroom.* Bloomington, IN: National Educational Service, 1992

Mendler, A. and Mendler, B. "Humor and Discipline," *Reclaiming Children and Youth,* 4(3), Fall 1995

Mendler, A. "Classroom Counteraggression," *Reclaiming Children and Youth,* 4(1), Spring 1995

Mendler, A. "Discipline with Dignity: An Approach for the 90's," *Learning,* January/February 1996

Wood, M. and Long, N. *Life Space Intervention.* Austin, TX: Pro-Ed, 1991